GOD
Thinks I Can Bench-Press a Buick

Cathy Sears

ISBN 979-8-89428-830-7 (paperback)
ISBN 979-8-89428-831-4 (digital)

Copyright © 2024 by Cathy Sears

All rights reserved. No part of this publication may be reproduced, distributed, or transmitted in any form or by any means, including photocopying, recording, or other electronic or mechanical methods without the prior written permission of the publisher. For permission requests, solicit the publisher via the address below.

Christian Faith Publishing
832 Park Avenue
Meadville, PA 16335
www.christianfaithpublishing.com

Printed in the United States of America

There is strength in numbers.

The girls:

Rhonda, Gwen, Sherry, Judy, Penny, Toni, Kym, Patty, Peggy, Susan

My gifts from God:

Danielle, Zachary, Jarrod, Mike

God Thinks I Can Bench-Press a Buick!

So I have always been told God will not give you more than you can handle. Somehow, I don't think that rule applies to me. Sit back, buckle up, and I'm gonna take you on a wild ride.

The Little River Town of Ludlow

IT ALL STARTS IN A small town along the banks of the Ohio River on the Kentucky side. The river was my backyard; our house sat right on the shore. I had the most wonderful childhood any little girl could want in this Mayberry-ish small town. Although, from my birth, there has been pain.

I was born on February 27, 1963. My maternal grandmother died thirty days after I was born. My dad's dad had died a year before that from an inoperable brain tumor. So my dad, a twenty-five-year-old young man, newly married, a veteran of the army with a new baby, was dealing with both his parents having passed away, knowing he had to raise his fourteen-year-old brother, John. Also, to stay in my grandparents' house, he had to get a mortgage and take over the house payments so everyone could stay in the house. My dad took John under his wing and finished raising him after my mama's death. My uncle John lived with us and is more like a big brother to me than an uncle. He eventually enlisted in the Air Force and was taken away to serve his country, of which I am very proud of him. He would always send me gifts from the different places he would go all over the world. After the Air Force, he moved back to the area he grew up in, got married, and eventually had three girls and one boy. I just lost my uncle John recently. He was a wonderful man.

My childhood was like a storybook. In the town that I grew up in, every family was friends with the other families. We ran the streets on our bicycles. My days pretty much consisted of getting up early, hopping on my bike, and running around our small town with all of my friends. The world was so different in the '60s and '70s. I was so lucky to grow up in this time and form long-lasting friendships.

Several of my girlfriends from high school, "the Girls," have a Christmas party every year, which started in our freshman year of high school in 1978. We still have our party to this day. Over the years, we have shared life's milestones. We went through years of college first, then marriages, divorces, babies, grandbabies, retirements, the deaths of spouses and our parents, and now retirement. They are my rock in times of need. We are all very close and support each other in every endeavor. I love them as if they were my blood sisters.

Whenever I speak to people from other areas, they are impressed that I even speak to anybody from high school. Our little town was different; our families all were friends. Our little town has a population of six thousand and a long history, being established in 1863. We are right across the river from Cincinnati and were a huge hub for the Underground Railroad during the Civil War.

For my eleventh birthday, I took my birthday money to the local pet shelter and adopted a rescue dog. He was a large black Irish wolfhound–Labrador mix, and I named him Henry. From the day I brought him home, he went to one part of my front yard and began to dig, and he dug, and he dug, and he dug. First, to stop him from digging, Dad placed a piece of chain-link fence over the top of the hole and a rock. The next morning, we woke up to find the chain-link fence had been removed, and he had continued to dig. The hole became so deep that my dad dropped large stones down to clog it up. One day, Dad went to drop large stones, and we heard a splash. The stones splashed into a water pool. We called the city to come down and find out what was under our yard. To our astonishment, he had opened up one of the underground tunnels that ran under the Ohio River for slaves to reach freedom in Cincinnati.

Rat with a Shotgun

YEARS BEFORE WE FOUND OUT about the tunnels for the Underground Railroad running under our property, there was one beautiful summer day. I was out in the side yard playing with my friend Melanie, whom my mom used to babysit because her mom had passed away. We were throwing rocks under the house, where there was a cinder block turned on its side in the foundation used as an air vent. Under our house was just a small dirt crawl space, so it was dark and damp and scary looking back into the cinder block.

After some time of playing this game, I started to throw another rock when, to my astonishment, out popped a double-barreled shotgun pointing straight at my nose. Melanie and I jumped and ran as quickly as we could to get to the house to tell my mom what had happened. Of course, I can't even imagine what my mom thought when we came in and told her this tall tale. An unbelievable story, but it is true. I saw that shotgun just as plain as day! Of course, the story got around my family, and I was always known as the little girl who saw a rat with a shotgun. As I sit here today, I swear I did see it, and it scared me to death.

I consider myself gifted with several blessings. I knew at an early age that I had something different from other people; I consider myself to be very sensitive. I can feel whether someone is a good person or not at the first meeting. I can walk through a home and feel different feelings in different rooms—heaviness on my chest, hard to breathe, coldness, and smells. Those are some of the feelings I experience.

I also learned at an early age that I have an artistic bone, with painting and sketching being my two favorite genres. When I'm painting, it's like I am somewhere far away and I don't think of any of the bad things that have happened to me in my life. I only think happy thoughts when I'm painting. My parents were very lenient when it came to my room, allowing me to do what I wanted. So every wall had different murals painted on them, such as album covers. The Bicentennial was a celebration we were dealing with in 1976. I had a life-size painting of Mickey Mouse dressed as George Washington on my wall in honor of the Bicentennial. I had Kiss's *Destroyer* album painted on my wall; they were my favorite band at the time. Kiss was my first concert too, before I discovered AC/DC.

I was somewhat of a savant when it came to trivia and knowledge of rock 'n' roll music, albums, lead singers, bands, etc. However, the stroke of 2022 erased all of this knowledge from my brain. I listen to songs now and don't even know what the song is, let alone who sang it. The brain is a funny thing.

My Best Friend

BEING AN ONLY CHILD, I suppose I was spoiled a little. But we were of very moderate means, and my dad worked very hard for what little we had. I grew up in my grandparents' house. My grandmother died thirty days after I was born, and my grandfather died one year earlier. So I did not know them, but I was always told lots of stories about their origins. These grandparents were of German descent, and I was always brought up recognizing our German heritage.

My dad was the best storyteller in the world. I was mesmerized by everything he talked to me about. He made every subject interesting, and I worshiped him. My dad was a huge sportsman and loved hunting and fishing. Unfortunately, all of his friends that he hunted with had boys, so it was a little awkward when he showed up with me. I grew up in a very tomboyish existence. I love hunting and fishing to this day; my dad instilled in me respect for Mother Nature and animals. We spent many days and late evenings in the woods together or on the bank of a farm pond.

My dad and I always had a very close and loving relationship. He certainly was always my rock, my first phone call when in need, my first phone call when I was crying. I jokingly tell everyone we were so close, he would stop and buy my tampons on the way home from work. My dad and I did everything together.

Tornado Alley

AROUND 1976, MY GIRL SCOUT troop went camping in Campbell County, Kentucky, at AJ Jolly Park. Sometime after dark, we were summoned to get out of the tents and retreat to the concrete block restroom building. We spent the rest of the night on the bathroom floor. The next morning, when it was light, we assessed the damage. Our tents and belongings were strewn across a large debris field. Our tents were destroyed, and we gathered up what we could find. Living in this area, we are familiar with tornadoes, but they don't get easier.

On April 3, 1974, tornado warnings were out. I was sitting at home with my dad when the tornado sirens went off around 2:00 p.m. My dad and I were watching out our back bedroom windows at the river for any activity because tornadoes were reported all over. Then the big one formed in Cincinnati, across the river from us. We saw a funnel cloud form on the banks of the river on the Ohio side. There it was, bouncing all over the bank, then it danced into the river, creating a large water spout. After that, it took off south down the river, creating major damage in its wake. It traveled to Sayler Park, Ohio, destroying everything in its path. It would take years to clean up the destruction.

March 11, 1986, was a day like any other. I was at work at Peoples Liberty Bank in Covington, Kentucky. Danielle and Zachary were at my dad's house about ten minutes away. Suddenly, we could hear strong storms outside. I was deep in the back of the bank with no windows, but we did have a back stairway door in our department. We opened the door, and water flooded our department. We ran to the front of the bank to see what was going on. We had huge glass windows in the front of the bank. I saw a Corvette sitting on the street in front of the bank; the wind lifted the front end up and slammed it back down violently. Someone went out and brought the driver back in. At this point, we were all hustled downstairs to our bomb shelter. There were people cut from flying glass. We waited there for what seemed like an eternity.

I had just purchased a newer car, which was parked in the back parking lot. Before we were released, we were told there was damage to the majority of cars in the parking lot. We were given the opportunity to make a phone call after they got us one line out. I called Dad, and he didn't know what I was talking about. He didn't see or hear anything. He was only a few miles away, which shows how tornadoes bounce around.

I came out and assessed the damage. There is a large domed Catholic church up the street that had the majority of the dome destroyed and scattered about. A large part of the copper dome roof was under my car. I had several windows broken. I hadn't even made my first payment. I drove home; it was complete chaos. We were on one corner, and there were three other banks on the other corners. Kentucky Governor Martha Layne Collins visited the area and sent the national guard in. For weeks afterward, we had to come to work to clean up. My department was getting ready to move to the newly renovated fourth floor, which was torn off!

Mamaw and Papaw

AT THE AGE OF SIXTEEN, my mom left the Appalachian Mountains to live with her cousin in the northern part of Kentucky. My mom's parents are the only grandparents I knew, and it was a wonderland to be in this part of Kentucky as a child. My cousins and I would play in the old broken-down cars that littered the yard, acting like we were racing each other in a NASCAR race. There were mountains to climb and old mines to explore. My grandpa was a coal miner and eventually died of black lung.

During the day, my mamaw would get a galvanized tub and place it on the side porch. Us kids would fill it up with water from the well, and then we were allowed to swim in it. We swam in it until it was time for Papaw and my uncles to come home from the mines. Then we were run out of the tub, and Papaw and my uncles would strip down to their underwear and scrub themselves from head to toe with a big ole cake of lye soap. Then we would all sit down and have a good dinner. Later, my family would play music out on the side porch until it was late and time to go to bed, and the day would start all over again the next day. I so looked forward to our visits, which were quite often. We only lived about three hours from my grandparents. I fell in love with these mountains when I was a little girl, and I knew eventually I would be back down here to live—and I am.

Being an only child, coming to Eastern Kentucky where I had a multitude of cousins to play with was always a lot of fun, great times, and fond memories. And the food! You have not eaten until you have eaten at the table of one of these beautiful mountain women down here.

My mom and I had a rough relationship. I always felt that she was jealous of my relationship with my dad. My mother is a hypochondriac; she has every medical disease there is. Two weeks after advertisements came out on restless leg syndrome, she had it. I always believed this was because she was fighting for my dad's attention. My mother had very few friends or interests outside the home. She was raised in the mountains by a very poor coal miner, his wife, and their twelve children. Her life mirrors the song "Coal Miner's Daughter." She was number 9 of 12. By the time she came along, I'm sure my grandma was worn out, and I believe my mother did not get the attention she always craved. She was raised very poor and left the mountains in 1958 to move to Northern Kentucky with her cousin.

That is when she met my dad, who had just gotten out of the army. My dad served six years in the army before I was born. He and Mom were married on April 12, 1960. On February 27, 1963, I came along. Thirty days later, on March 27, 1963, my dad lost his mother. He had a fourteen-year-old younger brother whom he had to take guardianship of. My dad was only twenty-five years old when all of this was dumped in his lap. Plus, he had to take over the mortgage to keep the house. That is a lot for a young man of only twenty-five in a short period of time. Sometimes I look at his life and see how it mirrors mine. I think I grew up accepting all trials in life. But my question has always been, when is enough?

We continued to live in that little town, and I graduated from high school in 1981. I married my high school sweetheart, Chip, and we immediately started a family. In other words, I was six months pregnant at the wedding.

Adulthood, Ugh

IN 1982, I WAS GIFTED with my beautiful daughter, Danielle. What a struggle it was to be an only child with no siblings, no grandparents, and suddenly, I had a baby. My daughter was followed by my son, Zachary, who was born in 1983. The following year, Chip and I divorced. So now, at twenty-one years old, I had two small children, thirteen months and three days apart, and I was on my own. This was a very difficult time in my life. Chip and I were young, and he had a menacing alcohol problem. As much as he tried to fight it, it was a demon that would not go away. We struggled terribly during the first year. It was a very difficult time, and we both tried the best we could.

The following year, my beautiful son was born after his sister. I struggled at first as a mother; being an only child, I had little access to childcare or experience with the responsibility of another small being. Our marriage was rocky from day 1 and led to divorce two years after our marriage. Now, not only was I a young mother, I was doing this on my own. I struggled to go to college, work full-time, and raise my two babies. For the most part, I believe they will tell you they had a wonderful childhood. My parents were a big part of that, as well as my ex-husband's family. I honestly don't think they wanted anything they did not get. It was a hard struggle, but that which does not kill us makes us stronger, right?

God has always played a huge part in my life. I was getting to the point that I was questioning my faith. I honestly thought I was being punished for mistakes I had made. It was about this time that I noticed bouts of severe "melancholy," as it was once known. I felt

God was giving me another challenge to overcome, and as usual, I buttoned down the hatches and worked hard to make it work. If only I had known at that time what my future was to hold.

Accident I

FIVE YEARS LATER, I DECIDED to try marriage again. This marriage was definitely a rebound. I thought I found someone who would not smack me around or drink too much. He turned out to be that, but he really didn't do much else. Full-time work was a struggle for him.

It was around this time that the first of multiple accidents we would have to deal with happened. It was a warm summer Friday, and it was Chip's weekend to get Danielle, six, and Zachary, five. He packed them up in his small yellow Datsun. They literally got about two miles from the house. We were getting ready to go visit friends when we heard sirens go down the main road past the house. We made a comment that it was a typical Friday evening. We went ahead to our friends' house and stayed until dark. Remember, this was before cell phones.

When we got home late, our neighbors were up and called us over to their house. To our shock, my mom had called them looking for us. We rushed to the hospital. By the time we got there, Danielle was prepped for surgery. Chip was screaming, and it was very chaotic. Danielle has a bad scar on her head to this day.

Evidently, Chip had come around a sharp bend in the road and met head-on with an oncoming car. The young man in the other car would eventually succumb to his injuries a week later. Chip had multiple injuries and was hospitalized. My sweet Danielle received a gnarly head injury with thirty staples in her head. She would have lingering effects from this injury. Thank God Zachary came through without any injuries.

Then I became pregnant with my third child, Jarrod. After finding out this news, I told his father he needed to get full-time work or leave. He was just another mouth to feed at this point. That was the last time we saw him. After four and a half years of my second marriage, he walked out because I told him he had to get continuous work. So now I am thirty-three, twice divorced, and a single parent of three children. I don't think anyone wakes up as a young child and says, "I want to be twice divorced and a single parent with three children." I wanted to live in a log cabin in the woods with no children or husband. But we play the hand that was dealt to us.

I always had support from my parents in every way. They were a huge part of my children's lives, helping with babysitting, food, and clothes. Things were certainly starting to change at this time in my life. I decided to make a career move. I worked for a new home builder in the office as a secretary. One day I was doing the sales managers' bonuses and thought to myself, *You know, I could do that. I could make this much money.* So I decided on a career change, and it was the best thing I ever did.

This job turned out to be the greatest thing that happened to me. Pretty instantly, my annual salary became three times what I had been accustomed to. I went through a wonderful time of great success. I met hundreds of wonderful people, and it was very fulfilling. During that time, my older two finished college. My daughter is a schoolteacher, my oldest son is an avionics mechanic, and my baby boy works at a large company. I could not be more proud of their lives. My children are successful and responsible.

The Accident II

ONE BEAUTIFUL JULY DAY, JARROD and I were invited to a farm picnic in Indiana, which we decided to attend. Jarrod was only nine years old. Once we arrived at the farm, we set up a small tent. Jarrod was sitting inside the tent playing with his G. I. Joe men, and I was outside talking with some of the ladies there. We didn't know anybody. I looked over to check on Jarrod to see if he needed anything, and he was gone. I stood up and started calling his name to see where he had gone. Maybe he was playing with some of the other little kids that were there?

Then mother's intuition overtook me. My heart dropped when I saw a young man coming toward me on the back of a four-wheeler. He was pointing at me and yelling to get my truck and come quickly; there had been an accident. I jumped in my truck and rode out to the end of the driveway, where I saw sheriffs' cars and heard an ambulance helicopter landing. Jarrod was lying in a creek bed on his back, and all I could see was his one leg bleeding profusely. He is highly allergic to poison ivy, and he landed in a big pile of it. The paramedics were working on him to get him stabilized and out of the creek bed to the helicopter ambulance. Evidently, one of the men had decided to give Jarrod a ride on a four-wheeler without asking permission.

Getting Jarrod out took quite a while, so I decided to walk over to see the condition of the man who had taken my son for a ride on a four-wheeler without my permission and caused a truck to wreck into them. I stood over him and looked at him while they worked on him on the blacktop. That's when I swung my leg back as far as it would go, and I threw the most powerful kick to his head that I could muster. He had hurt my baby, and I was devastated.

Eventually, Jarrod was put into the helicopter. The ambulance drivers and EMT told me I would have to get in my truck and drive to Cincinnati Children's Hospital to meet them there. This was about an hour-and-a-half drive. I looked at them and said, "You have got to be kidding me. This helicopter is not leaving this ground without me on it with my son." I was told they weren't allowed to carry pedestrians, only injured people. There was a weight limit on the helicopter. I told the EMTs that they would have to stay and drive to Cincinnati because I was going in the helicopter with my son. After some deliberation, it was agreed that I would ride in the helicopter to Children's Hospital in Cincinnati. I got a jump seat, and they strapped me in with a five-point harness, and off we flew.

I don't remember a lot about the flight. I just remember I was terrified because I was afraid to fly anyway. Let alone in this situation in a helicopter. Jarrod was unconscious, so he does not remember any of the flight or the landing. Later, after he was well, we were invited to come back and visit the tower and let him get his wings, which we did.

We landed on top of the hospital on the helicopter pad, and all I saw were hundreds of white coats running toward me. In the middle of all the white coats, I saw a priest. He immediately made his way over to me and told me he would be my liaison between my family and notifying whoever I needed to notify. I told him, "Father, I appreciate your help, but right now I don't want to notify anybody. There is no father. I have no siblings, no grandparents. I will notify my parents when I'm ready to."

It seemed like an eternity before they took Jarrod into the ER and prepped him for surgery. We were up all night, waiting for him to go into surgery for the first time. Before his first surgery, we were put into a waiting room with the lights out. It was about one o'clock in the morning when Jarrod looked at me over my shoulder and said, "I love you, Papaw."

I said, "Papaw is not here." About that time, I felt a hand on my shoulder. Mom and Dad had heard the news on the local news station and knew it was us, so they came to Children's Hospital in the middle of the night.

Jarrod stayed at Children's Hospital for approximately three months. There were multiple surgeries. The final tally of all the injuries included a broken anterior clavicle, broken femur, growth plate, pelvis, tibia, and fibula. Along with broken bones, there were multiple areas that needed plastic surgery to fix. Rehabilitation would take years. To this day, he can tell you days before it rains. I worked out of his hospital room, thank God for my company allowing me to do this. Again, I was on my own, dealing with a major setback for my poor son. I will go to my grave with guilt for having him at this party.

Upon his release from the hospital, we had to set up his homeschooling and a home health-care nurse, who came during the week to change his bandages and bring his schoolwork. At the time, we had a harlequin Great Dane named Duke, and he was crazy about Jarrod. He would not let anyone around him. When the teacher and nurse came over, I had to put Duke in the bedroom. He was quite a big boy, standing about 6 feet tall and weighing about 180 pounds, so he was quite intimidating, but he was just a big baby.

Moving On

AFTER SEVERAL YEARS OF BEING single, I met Kevin. Kevin came into our lives at a point when I was ready for him, and he was ready for me. Kevin had once been divorced with no children and had a great job at the local airport working for Comair. Kevin and I hit it off from the beginning; he was a deeply loving and caring individual.

Kevin stepped right into the role of stepdad for Jarrod, who was only nine, along with my older grown children. Kevin fit right into the family, and everybody loved him. Kevin and I had been together for ten years when our great life came crashing to a halt.

It was 2008—the market had crashed! Kevin lost his job with Comair after seventeen and a half years, and it devastated him. His mental health started deteriorating. In 2010, I lost my job in my dream career due to the recession and the falling market in the housing industry. I had been there for twenty years. I was devastated and lost.

Since I was in commissioned sales, I was not eligible for unemployment benefits. I burned through my savings and stocks pretty quickly. Kevin got his CDL license and began driving a truck.

Camp

MY COUSIN INVITED US TO visit her at a campground on the Ohio River named River Ridge, where she had purchased a camper. Kevin and I went to visit and instantly fell in love with the campground. Nothing would satisfy us until we had a camper of our own there. We immediately started looking for campers and found one in Georgia that fit our needs. We had it transported to Northern Kentucky to the campground.

Kevin and I made many friends and had a great time there for twelve years. After Kevin died, I tried to go back and enjoy the campground, but it was just not the same. There were some great friends there and some very unpleasant people. After Kevin passed away and I decided to move to Eastern Kentucky, I was informed that the annual fee setup had changed to quarterly. I was fine with that and, in the process of moving to Eastern Kentucky, called to make arrangements to meet someone to help me hook up my camper. I wanted to pay my dues and settle my bill. To my astonishment, I discovered that the president of the campground had my camper removed because I hadn't paid the $350 fee on time, even after being a customer for twelve years. This happened shortly after Kevin passed away. This is how cruel some people can be. To this day, I have no clue where my camper went. Then they sued me for the $350 fee, which I never paid. This was truly heartbreaking. I had considered the majority of the people in that camp to be very close friends. I do miss the camp; it was a great social event each weekend. I'm truly sorry that a few people had to do this to me. Kevin and I had just bought that camper and paid $6,000 for it. To this day, I have no clue where it is.

One of my many pastimes at camp was fishing at the river. It was not unusual to see me down there at all hours of the night on the banks, with my two poles in the water, searching for that big catfish. One particular night, I put the poles in around ten o'clock in the evening and fished until all hours of the morning. Then my phone rang around 4:00 a.m. I jumped and answered it; it was my son. He had been out with friends and had just returned home to find the front door standing wide open. I told him to get out of the house, go to the neighbors, and call the police. I jumped in my car and took off home. By the time I got there, the state police wouldn't arrive for another two hours.

After the detective finished his report, I decided to go into the house and see how bad it was. It was as you can imagine. My bedroom was the worst. They had emptied my walk-in closet and my dresser onto the bedroom floor. They had taken my mattress and box springs off my bed. My computers were all gone. Ironically, they did not take one television. It took days to clean up the mess, and then I had to take an inventory of all the items that were missing. I did not have major jewelry pieces, but I did have a few rings that meant a lot to me, including my class ring, which was taken.

They had gained entry from throwing a rock out of my landscaping through the sliding glass door at the back of the house. So now I had to replace the sliding glass door, which I told my son we would do. We did go buy a new sliding glass door and replace the old one.

Government Conspiracy

ONE MORNING, KEVIN WOKE ME up, telling me that the government had tapped into our cell phones and computers. It was about 8:00 a.m., and he had already been to the phone company to complain, with no result. He came home, roused me out of bed, and told me I needed to go with him since I was the signer on the account. I got dressed, and we went to the phone company.

When I walked in the door, all the employees looked over at us, and I knew something bad had occurred earlier that morning. A man headed toward us, introduced himself as the manager, and took us into his office. The manager explained to me that Kevin had been there earlier regarding people tapping into our phones. He tried to explain to me that the situation Kevin had in his head was not reality. I agreed and shuffled Kevin out the door to the car. I explained to him that there was nothing going on with our phones, but he was headstrong in the belief that somebody was tapping into our phones and talking to him through the radio.

I knew things were really bad at that point. I drove him straight to his parents' house and pulled his mother into the back bedroom to tell her what had happened and asked her to call the squad. Kevin refused to go to the hospital on his own, so we had to call the life squad. You can imagine how horrible that was! He did go willingly with the police and life squad to the emergency room, where he was admitted into the psychiatric unit that day.

After his release, he seemed to do a little better on new medication for a while. But then things turned around, and they started getting worse again. He could hear voices talking to him. I accompanied him to his doctors' offices and appointments and tried to help out as much as I could. I was in another situation where I had no idea what to do; this was way above my pay grade. Kevin tried hard to deal with his mental issues, but they continually interfered with his daily life. This time was a significant struggle for both of us.

My Pony

AFTER THE COLLEGES WERE FINISHED, I decided to reward myself with a 2008 Mustang convertible GT with all the extras. I think we all dream of a certain car we would like to have, and this one had been my favorite! Not only did I buy this Mustang brand-new, but I also had $10,000 in aftermarket options put on. This car went away for storage in the winter and only saw sunny, hot, dry days. You could say I was a little obsessed with her. I never had a brand-new car, and this was my dream car. I kept my old truck for everyday use, so she had very little mileage.

Have you ever heard the old adage, "When things feel too good, something bad is going to happen?" Well, after a day of hunting with my dad in 2009, he became very ill. Now I am talking about a man who never took an aspirin. He woke up and was very confused all of a sudden. I got the dreadful call from my mom, pleading for help with him. I went down to see him and tried to get him to go to the hospital. Stubborn as he was, we went back and forth, and finally, I had to say, "We can do this the easy way or the hard way. I will call the ambulance, and the neighbors will see you come out and get into the ambulance, or you can get in my car and let me drive you."

That drive to the hospital, approximately fifteen minutes, plays over and over again in my head. For the first time, I hollered at my own dad. At the hospital, we were told he had cirrhosis of the liver with hepatic encephalopathy (HE). Cirrhosis is a hardening, so you can get cirrhosis of anything. Cirrhosis of the liver is stereotypically associated with alcoholics, but my dad was anything but an alcoholic. He drank in his early days while in the army, but it had been years since liquor touched his lips. His cirrhosis was from Tylenol and aspirin. This disease has very few cures. I watched him decline, losing his memory and experiencing dementia-like episodes. He had to be on medication that caused constant diarrhea, and I watched him humiliated by the situation.

One day, while I was at their house, Mom told me stories of him almost hitting people on the road when he was driving. Unfortunately, being an only child puts you in a position of no vice president. I had to make the decision to take his car keys away and sell his truck. That was the second worst day of my life. I watched him look into my eyes and cry because he knew he would never get them back. I looked at him and saw a young version of my dad when he took my keys away. He was done at that point, I knew in my heart.

Accident III

ON A BEAUTIFUL NOVEMBER DAY, I was headed to get my dad and take him to the VA for his medicine. It was a gorgeous, sunny day. I had the top down on the Mustang, a big pot of soup beans in the backseat for Mom and Dad, and the radio was blasting the Bee Gees song "Stayin' Alive." In front of me on the expressway, the traffic had come to a stop, so I did too.

Those seconds go over again in my mind; it seemed like an eternity. I glanced up in the rearview mirror out of habit and saw a flash of a large truck coming straight toward me at a high rate of speed. You hear stories of people saying their lives flash before their eyes, and that's exactly what happened. I saw my children as small babies and saw myself as a young girl swinging in the backyard in front of the river. All of those stories are true.

All the other lanes were packed, so there was nowhere for him to go except to hit me, which in turn pushed me into the SUV in front of me, then projected me off into the emergency lane to hit the wall. My beautiful car was broken in half. I was in shock. A huge semi drove up by where I was and shouted out, "Move your damn car!" I remember thinking to myself how evil someone could be; I was sitting there in a destroyed car, blood on my face, and that was the best thing he could think to say?

The lady in the SUV in front of me came back to see how I was doing. She was crying hysterically because she had a two-year-old little boy in the backseat of her SUV. I remember thinking to myself that God put me between that SUV and that truck to save that baby's life. If I had not been there, that baby would've been killed.

I did not go to the hospital that night, I believe I was just in shock and wanted to go home. That night was horrific; I was in pain all evening. Early the next morning, I woke up and had Kevin take me to the emergency room.

Kevin and I had been together for thirteen years, and he was very kind and good to me. I had multiple muscular trauma, a broken right foot, and a head injury. Who knew the airbags would not work unless the car hit at a certain angle? I learned so much after this accident. I was sent home and had to come back for multiple months for therapy and a cast on my foot.

During that time, Kevin started having psychological episodes. He had also lost his job at the airport, a huge employer in our area. After the loss, he started spiraling down a bad mental path. Kevin did not take drugs and was not an alcoholic by any means. There was just some wiring that was crossed in his brain, and I could tell. As I was trying to recuperate from my car accident, I had to ask Kevin to stay with his parents for a few days because he was making scary choices. Kevin was on medication, but unbeknownst to me, he had stopped taking it.

Kevin drove a truck and had to have his yearly physical. They sent him to a doctor who had never seen him, and this doctor told him he could not drive a truck on that medication. So now he thought he was going to lose another job. I honestly believe this is what pushed him over the edge. Things got pretty bad, and I needed him to stay at his mom's until I got well. I was on the mend for about two weeks.

My youngest son, Jarrod, and his wife and son, Ares, were living with me temporarily. They had found an apartment to move into, so they stopped by to drop off Ares. He was going to stay with me for a little while so they could move their things to the new place. I love my grandchildren and enjoy every opportunity to have them visit. Now that they are moving into their own apartment, I will be alone and will miss them terribly.

That morning, I got out of bed, and my right arm was numb. I walked into the living room and tried to speak but could not. Something was wrong! I could not say a full sentence. Ironically, I had just gotten a magnet for my refrigerator at Kroger's that showed the five signs of a stroke. I took my son to the magnet and pointed at it.

He said, "You think you're having a stroke?"

I shook my head yes, and we got in the car fast. Jared took me to the hospital, and sure enough, I was having a stroke, so I was admitted. My speech and the feeling in my right arm returned the next day. Happily, I was told this was a dissolving clot. I dodged yet another bullet of a brain bleed. They kept me in the hospital another day, then released me.

This is when it gets really intense. Put on your seatbelts because it's going to be a rocky ride.

Leaving the hospital, I stopped at the grocery to get a few things. In the midst of shopping, my phone rang with the distinctive ring of Kevin. I thought to myself, *Oh, I will call him later when I get home.* I think back on that moment almost daily. What if I would have answered the phone? What if he was calling me for help? I guess I will never know. I was in the middle of the grocery store, you know.

After checking out, I drove straight home, and my evening was very calm. When I got home, Jarrod told me that Kevin had stopped by and said he would see us tomorrow on Thanksgiving at Danielle's house. I would later find out this was when he went into my bedroom and got my pistol out of my nightstand. I took a good shower, fixed myself a little drink, and watched television until I normally went to bed. At some point, off to bed, I went.

My daughter-in-law and grandson were still living at my house; they had not completely moved yet. I remember hearing her voice calling me, but I was in a deep sleep. Then I heard her say, "The police are here, and they want to talk to you." Now, my family is the most law-abiding people in the world. We do not break laws. So the first thing that came to my mind was, my dad had passed away. I got out of bed and walked into my dining room, where two uniformed officers were standing there staring at me.

I looked at them and said, "What can I do for you?" The Kenton County officers told me that I should sit down. I told them I did not want to sit down, but they insisted. Then one of the officers looked at me and asked, "Do you know a Kevin Luster?"

I fell to the ground. I just knew something bad had happened. I said, "Yes, has he been in an accident?"

The officer looked at me and said, "No, he is deceased. I cannot tell you anything about it, but a detective will be calling you soon to discuss the details." They went to the door and left, and that was the last I saw of them—totally emotionless, nonempathetic, cold transaction.

I sat by myself and cried for hours. About two hours later, a detective called and told me Kevin had been found in the woods with a single gunshot wound to his head. I said, "Where in the woods?"

He said, "Stephenson Road, do you know anybody on that road?"

I replied, "No." Then I got to thinking, we own a piece of land on that road, just land, no house.

Then he asked, "Does he have access to a .38 handgun?"

I said, "No." Then I remembered I had a .38 caliber handgun and asked him to hold on. I ran into my room and pulled out my nightstand drawer, and my pistol was gone.

Kevin had to have stopped by the house that day; that was when he called me, and I did not answer the phone. Now I have to live with that for the rest of my life. What would have happened if I had answered the phone? Maybe he just wanted to talk to me, and I could've talked him out of it? Empty, empty, empty questions riddle my mind. The next day was Thanksgiving. Thanks to Kevin, Thanksgiving will always be remembered as the day he committed suicide.

I have never known anyone who has committed suicide. The pain that he felt shifted to me. The pain is indescribable. I closed my eyes and visualized the scene. I wonder what his last thoughts were before he pulled the trigger. I can't believe that I was so insensitive that I let it get to this point. Am I that selfish person my mother always told me I was? Nobody knows the gut-wrenching, burning pain. I never realized how physical the pain could get. I didn't sleep much for months after this. I tried to put different ideas in my mind, but they wouldn't stick.

I am a Catholic, so I sought out counseling from my church. The priest gave me a new Bible and told me he would pray for me; that was about the extent of it. Really, no one can make the pain go away. It is something like the flu that has to run its course. How long? I don't believe there is a time limit on mourning. I do remember the very first day that I woke up and my stomach didn't hurt. It was about eight months later. I remember the wonderful, overwhelming feeling of contentment in not having that pain, just for a few minutes.

I had been working with an attorney on my disability right before the car accident. I immediately made an appointment to go in and talk to him about representing me for the car accident. Meeting with him and answering his questions about the details started a lawsuit, and I was really hoping I could get another replacement car. Then I told him of the devastating suicide by Kevin, and we talked in his office for quite some time. I told him that Kevin's employer had contacted me and that he had a life insurance policy, but it was void due to suicide. My attorney told me that was not true. He looked into it, sent one letter, and the insurance company agreed to pay me the life insurance policy of $150,000. My attorney told me that he got one-third for writing the one letter and it only took one week to receive. I thought to myself, that's a pretty good way to make a living. I thought it was a little unfair also. But what was I supposed to do? I had to have legal counsel to get through losing my job because I had been hospitalized, help me get disability, work on the car accident, and help me with the life insurance policy. Needless to say, my file got pretty thick with the attorney.

Over a four-year period, the attorney badgered me to get extensive medical treatment, which I did not have the money to do, and to go to therapy and a doctor once a week, which I also did not have the money to do. He would get frustrated with me and be very nasty to me. He was an older gentleman in his late seventies and showed signs of dementia and short-term memory loss. Our relationship got very sticky when I decided to move to the mountains, which was only a three-hour drive, and I could return at any time to meet with him, but that was not good enough. He wanted to meet three or four times a week in his office and discuss nothing.

By the time it came to settle my car accident, three and a half years later, I received a copy of a court document that removed him as my counsel. I had no idea what this meant. So I called his office, and his secretary told me I needed to get a new attorney to settle my case. Have you ever had an attorney in a car accident, and they dismissed themselves as your counsel all the way through, almost to the end? It is impossible to get another attorney to take your case. I searched for months, being turned down by every attorney I spoke with. Nobody wants to pick up another attorney's mess. I finally did find one attorney who said he would help me settle the case. The case originated at $150,000 in settlement. The new attorney told me I would be lucky to get $10,000. I had already paid $10,000 in medical bills out of my own pocket, but he told me that was not retrievable.

After the insurance adjuster met with us, it was a complete nightmare. After three and a half years, they broke me down and had me sobbing in the office, and I walked out with a check for $3,000. No replacement car, no medical bill reimbursements, no place in my life back to the moments before the car accident. My original attorney retired and now lives in a beautiful condo in Florida. I attempted to file a suit against him through the Kentucky attorney's office, and they responded that I had no merit. How does this happen to somebody? You hear stories of people getting half a million or a quarter million dollars in settlement for car wrecks where they're hit from the rear end while sitting still. I left out in debt. This is my luck. How does this happen to somebody? How could somebody's luck be so bad that even justified acknowledgment is out of the question? Again, I ask myself, what did I do to deserve this? I worked my whole life for this damn car, and I walked away owing money and no car for something I had no control over, a blatant accident. There was no question who was at fault; the other driver was cited at the scene. Yet here I am again? And I asked myself, *Am I cursed? This does not happen to other people!*

The days later were long. Honestly, I don't remember the majority of them. I continued to work with my dad and help him and get him anything he needed. Now, going from one tragedy to the inevitable keeps my mind busy. My dad continued to spiral downward. I had accepted what was going to happen. After watching him plummet physically and mentally, I was ready for him to be in peace. That does not mean it wasn't going to hurt all over again, but with him, I had a little time to prepare. I got the dreaded phone call at 5:00 a.m. from my mother. She called to tell me he was having another episode, and she was taking him to the ER. I knew in my gut this was the last trip. His body had been devastated by this disease; he could barely walk, he had lost a considerable amount of weight, and his skin was hanging. They admitted him to the ICU, and we never had a discussion after that. They put him into a medically induced coma, then on kidney dialysis. This blew him up like a balloon.

After a few days, the doctors admitted there was no more they could do. My mother made the decision to remove the equipment. My dad's brother, who is a Baptist, had his preacher come in. I, as a Catholic, summoned the hospital priest. We stayed with him for about eight hours until he passed away. It had been ten months since Kevin had passed. Dad was ready, and he wanted to go so badly. I know he's in heaven with his mom and dad. That gives such great comfort. I know he and Kevin are hunting and fishing in heaven.

I went through a great amount of time being alone. My mind would burn with pain. I questioned my creator, "Why are you giving me so many crosses to bear? Am I cursed?" I even contacted a spiritualist to do a cleansing of evil spirits and curses. I was desperate for some calm, peace, and painlessness. I frequently leaned on alcohol; it cleared my mind of all the pain. I still get the vision of Kevin sitting in the woods against a tree with his brains blown out. How do you erase that from your mind? Alcohol. Drinking certainly is not the answer, but when you have no siblings or grandparents to lean on, what do you do? People judged me, but that's the cross they have to bear. I didn't care if anybody judged me; it took the ever-playing movie out of my mind. Eventually, the alcohol wasn't enjoyable, so I turned to cannabis. I love smoking pot. Judge me if you will, but it really does numb the mind. Memories play over in my mind like movies, and sometimes I just need a commercial break.

I'm Not an Only Child Anymore

AFTER A YEAR OF REDEFINING myself and rethinking my life, I decided to do something I always wanted to do: run away to the Appalachian Mountains of Eastern Kentucky, where my family is. We often visited here when I was young, and I have many cousins here whom I love deeply. It's really the only family I ever had besides my parents.

One thing I had always been intrigued by was the Native American culture and ancestry that my mamaw said we had. I was always told we had Native American blood in our line, but I was never sure how much or where it came from. Now, in 2017, you can pay a fee and get your DNA tested. Who would've thought? So I was excited to order my ancestry test to see if it showed any native blood.

A few weeks later, I received the results. I couldn't find any Sears relatives or any of my German heritage on my dad's side. I was a little confused about how to read the results. It showed I had very little German ancestry. Basically, what they do is take everybody's DNA results and put them into a big bank. When new people get a DNA test, it matches everybody out there who has ever taken the test before. They list these matches from the closest match down. At the top of my list were two ladies, Theresa and Melissa. The test results said they were my first cousins or closer. Now what does that mean? I didn't know these ladies. I know every first cousin I have. I have sixty-five first cousins, and I know each one of them. I did not know these two ladies.

They give you an option to contact them, so we corresponded for several months, but none of us could figure this out. Then Melissa, who is a PRN, offered to get an outside lab DNA test that is specifically for siblings. Of course, I laughed and said, "I can tell you both right now my mom or dad never messed around." Isn't that what we all think?

So I received my DNA test in the mail, did my swab, mailed it back to Canada, and we waited. Then I got a text from Melissa that said, "Hello, sister." I ran to the mailbox, and my results were in there. These two ladies are my half-sisters. I got back in my truck and just cried. I beat the steering wheel and the dashboard, then I got sick, opened my door, and threw my guts up. I sat there for quite a while until I could compose myself enough to drive back home. I had lost my dad all over again. It was just like he died once again, and now I had to accept the fact that his blood was not running through my veins. Not only am I not German, but I am not his daughter. The pain is indescribable now.

How do you swallow this information? How do you take this in and accept it? How am I supposed to accept this and move on? How much is too much? Why am I given these crosses to bear? I am fifty-five years old, and I am to accept the fact that my mother had an affair three years into their marriage, which produced me. Me, my dad's only daughter and only child. Me, who grew up with two loving parents in the most wonderful childhood any child could ask for. What do I do now? How am I supposed to process this in my brain and live a normal life again? At this point, my life will never be normal again. Floods of memories come into my brain, memories of my dad and the fact that he was lied to for fifty-five years and went to his grave not knowing the truth. I don't know if I'm angrier at my mother for lying to me or lying to my father.

My entire life, my mother had very few friends and went nowhere without me or my dad. My mother didn't even drive until I turned sixteen and got my license. My mother had no social life; she didn't start working outside the house until my late teens. How could this happen? How could this lie have been carried on this long? How could she have kept this inside? There are too many questions to answer, so my mind periodically shuts down. Am I cursed? I honestly believe that somewhere in my past, someone has put a curse on me. I guess I'm just trying to find a logical reason for why so many things have happened to me in a short period of time. Why does the universe, a higher being, call it what you like, disperse so much negative energy to one person in a short period of time? I ask myself daily, *What do I do now? Now that I know the truth of this horrid lie?* This is a burden I will carry to my grave; the pain will not stop until my heart quits beating. My dad has been so disrespected by a stupid young person's mistake or choice.

Focusing on my new life of having siblings, my kids now have aunts, uncles, and cousins. Recently, we discovered a new sister who was given up for adoption. She lives in Arizona and is a nurse. We are just beginning to build a relationship with her. Of the four, two sisters were given up for adoption; she is one of them.

I discovered that I not only have four half-sisters, Theresa, Melissa, Rafika, and Sue, but two half-brothers, David and Lon. The original two sisters have been fabulous. Theresa and Melissa have the same mother, who had a romantic relationship with the sperm donor, but he wanted her to give them up for adoption, and she was smart enough not to do that. God sent me warm and accepting sisters, more than I could have imagined. They have known their whole life who their sperm donor was. I refer to him as the sperm donor because I do not want to know him, I do not want him to know me, and I want nothing from him or his family. To me, he is a drop of blood and that is it.

Daniel Boone and Native Americans

A MAJOR DISCOVERY IN MY ANCESTRY results revealed that Daniel Boone is my fifth great-uncle. Daniel's brother, Israel Boone, is my fifth great-grandfather. While Daniel and Israel were leading settlers through the Cumberland Gap down the Wilderness Trail in 1775, on the other side of my heritage are Native Americans who were also my ancestors.

Chief Redbird Aron Brock, of the Redbird area in Kentucky, is one of them. The Redbird River is said to have run red when Chief Redbird was massacred. Chief Redbird's grandson is George Goldenhawk Sizemore. Goldenhawk had fifty-four to fifty-seven children in the Magoffin County area and was arrested for bigamy. He claimed head of household for multiple families in the 1900 census. He came over to Floyd County and hooked up with my mamaw.

If you are a Sizemore from Eastern Kentucky, I guarantee we are related. There is a website dedicated to him and a monument in Salyersville, Kentucky, honoring him as the "Father of Magoffin County." They say if every descendant contributed $1, they could build a large monument.

The Dreaded Confrontation

NOW IT WAS THAT TIME I had dreaded. I knew it was time to sit my mother down. I knew it wasn't going to amount to much; we never had a warm and fuzzy relationship. We were never very close or shared intimate secrets like most mothers and daughters do. But I knew she loved me, and I loved her in our way.

    I confronted my mother and made time to sit down and have a deep conversation with her. This did not turn out anything like I expected. My mother has always been very introverted and quite a narcissist. In her eyes, she does no wrong and never has. In her eyes, she was a loving wife, mother, and wonderful grandmother. The truth of the matter is, she was a wonderful grandmother, and I was very lucky to have her help in raising my kids. In the mothering field, she could've used some help. Of course, I see things completely differently; I was on the opposing end of her affection.

    I took pictures of my two sisters and the DNA test results to meet with her. I said, "Mother, I have to ask you a very serious question: why do these girls look like me?" She glanced across my computer screen at the pictures. Without taking any time to look closely, she responded with, "I don't know." I carried on to the DNA results. I explained to her that people are sent to prison based on DNA and that it was scientific proof that these two women were my sisters.

    There was a silence in the room for a split second, then she said, "Put that silly stuff down and come in here to the kitchen and get some brownies. Those tests are stupid, and I don't know why you waste your time on them. Your dad is your dad!" That was the last we discussed it. I figured, why go any further? She was seventy-six years old and had kept the lie for fifty-seven years. I think after you keep a lie that long, it becomes the truth. I knew from that moment I was not going to get any healing through her. She has to carry that burden now until she dies, that I know!

I asked the usual questions: "Were you raped?"

She laughed and responded, "Don't you think I would know if I was raped?" That tells me she was not assaulted. I have come to terms with whatever happened. I'm not interested in the details. I guess I just wanted confirmation. I guess I will go to my grave without confirmation.

2024

So that should catch you up on where I am today. How do you go on living with a horrible lie, a devastating suicide, car accidents, and horrifying strokes? After each trial in my life, I have always looked to God for salvation, but I ask now: is God enough?

Every day I wake up, and all of this is on my mind. At times, I just want a vacation away from the thoughts, so I drink and indulge in cannabis. I have wonderful friends and sisters, but it doesn't seem to be enough. What is enough? When is too much?

Years ago, I did think about taking my own life, but after Kevin's suicide, I see how horrible it is. I don't want that to be my legacy to my children, grandchildren, and future grandchildren. I don't want to be the one who committed suicide.

So at this point in my life, I ask, now what? Do I just swallow it deep and deal with it? No. I thought I would write a book to get this out of my chest and hopefully help somebody else out there who is going through multiple traumas and just does not know how to handle it. I certainly do not have the answers, but I do have a lot of life experiences to share.

I did contact the Dr. Phil show. I was looking for any type of help I could get. My children were not happy with that because they do not want our personal business hung out on the line. But since I am the victim, not them, I make the choice of what happens to me. The Dr. Phil show obviously was not interested in my story, and that is okay also.

So now what? Where do I go from this point on? I wish there was a magic pill that I could swallow and wake up and everything would be gone. But that's not reality. I have to deal with it one-on-one, day by day, situation by situation. It takes a toll on you. I'm not the strong person I used to be. I'm very mellowed and somewhat defeated. All of this feels like you've lost a major battle, and you're just supposed to keep it quiet and suck it up. That's easier said than done.

Who do you lean on? Who do I tell every day how much the pain hurts? I had a friend tell me one time that it makes you feel better when you release all of your pain because it is like puking, but it also makes everyone around you sick from listening to it. So who do you talk to?

I tried my priest; that did not turn out like I wanted it to. I set up a meeting with Father, and when I got there, I told him what all I had been going through.

He said, "Let's bow our heads, and pray together." Then he looked at me and handed me a Bible and told me good luck. So I left.

My close friends, I'm sure, are sick of hearing about it. My family doesn't want me to disrespect my mom in any way. Never mind what I'm going through. The doctors continue to throw pills at me to erase my thoughts and pain, but it does not go away. It will never go away. That is the reality, so I have to learn how to deal with it. I need to put it in a place where it's not constantly a burden on my shoulders. I have enough burdens to deal with until the day I close my eyes forever. Nobody can take this pain away. Nobody can snap their fingers and rearrange everything back to 2012.

So it is up to me to figure out a way to keep myself occupied, busy, and continually healing for the rest of my life. Talk about a job!

HOW MUCH IS TOO MUCH? Did you ever experience a trauma in your life and wonder to yourself, *Why did this happen to me?* Do you ever feel like there's a curse on you? What did you do in this life or a previous one that caused you to be punished now? Am I cursed? What did I ever do to cause such deep, gut-wrenching, life-changing pain? Does the pain ever go away? Is this something I'm going to have to live with for the rest of my life? What in the hell did I do?

I've always tried hard to be kind to other people, to be giving, to be loving, and to do what God taught me I should do. And for that, I'm being punished? Over and over in my mind, I try to figure out what I did and how I can change it. When I tell people what I've been through, they usually just shake their heads, and there is no comforting response.

Then I think, what about all the people in the world who have had worse traumas and tragedies than me? I wonder what happened in their previous lives. I watch the news and see horrific tragedies happen to other people, and then I feel selfish. Selfish that I am sitting around feeling sorry for myself because of my traumas, which do not compare to the woman who lost both her twin sons in a car accident or to the couple whose house burned down, losing everything. Is that how we are punished? Do we bring those negativities to our new lives when we are born?

I've spent the majority of my adult life trying to redo my wrongs, hoping this will bring positive luck. I will do anything to take the pain away. But the pain never seems to go away. It doesn't disappear;

it gets put on a shelf in my mind. I won't forget the pain, and I still feel the pain, but it is much easier to deal with as time goes forward.

I surround myself with a small circle of the right people, those who are positive and I know have my back. I always knew I could count on the girls. I always knew I could count on my three kids and my husband, Mike. I have seven awesome grandbabies, six boys and one granddaughter. Things have gotten less stressful now that I have moved to the mountains. It is very, very therapeutic to have somebody else in your life. Mike, coming into my life in such a stressful time, has made me appreciate him even more.

I can happily say today that I do deal with the pain on a daily basis, but it does not ruin or run my life. I am very happy. I am in a good place. Mike and I just bought a new home. Our home is up a holler in the mountains in Hazard, Kentucky. We have mountains wrapped all the way around us, full of beautiful, lush woods, plenty of wildlife, ponds, and creeks. It is a paradise here. Our dogs live in doggy paradise. We are in a good place, both of us, and we're very happy. We have a very loving family. Mike has three children of his own, and along with my three, we sound like the Brady Bunch.

It has taken a long time to get to this place, so if you're dealing with any type of situation of your own, just remember one day it will calm down. There is no set time limit on pain. The best thing I can suggest is that you talk to somebody, whether it be your priest, preacher, best friend, sibling, parent, or grandparent…somebody.

About the Author

I WAS BORN IN 1963 IN a small, picturesque river town along the Kentucky side of the Ohio River. My relationship with God started early in my life, although my parents didn't go to church. Over the years, multiple tragedies have tested that relationship, I must confess. Yet I always come back and lean on my faith. My faith has pulled me through each trauma.